TRAGEDY AND TRIUMPH

FIND HIM FAITHFUL

AN AUTOBIOGRAPHY

J. Dale Alderfer

TRILOGY CHRISTIAN PUBLISHERS
TUSTIN, CA

Trilogy Christian Publishers
A Wholly Owned Subsidary of Trinity Broadcasting Network
2442 Michelle Drive
Tustin, CA 92780

For information, address Trilogy Christian Publishing

Rights Department, 2442 Michelle Drive, Tustin, Ca 92780.

Trilogy Christian Publishing/ TBN and colophon are trademarks of Trinity Broadcasting Network.

For information about special discounts for bulk purchases, please contact Trilogy Christian Publishing.

Manufactured in the United States of America

10 9 8 7 6 5 4 3 2 1

Library of Congress Cataloging-in-Publication Data is available.

ISBN 978-1-64773-588-3

ISBN 978-1-64773-589-0 (ebook)

Contents

Preface

My motivation and purpose for writing and sharing my story is out of obedience to what I believe God has called me to do, and to point all to Jesus Christ, the author and finisher of my faith. My heart's desire is to clearly present the gospel, which provides the foundation on which we build our lives every day. I want all to know our Savior's love for us, and that He will never leave us or forsake us (Hebrews 13:5), no matter our current experience or circumstance, whether in tragedy or triumph. My aspiration is to share my life and the reality of Romans 8:28 (NKJV), "And we know that all things work together for good to those who love God, to those who are called according to His purpose," and to be that individual who lives out 2 Corinthians 1:3-4 (NKJV), "Praise be to the God and Father of our Lord Jesus Christ, the Father of compassion and the God of all comfort, who comforts us in all our troubles, so that we can comfort those in any trouble with the comfort we ourselves receive from God." This is all for the glory of our God and Savior, Jesus Christ.

J. DALE ALDERFER

Acknowledgements

There are so many that I am eternally grateful for and to, for the input and for blessing me on my life's journey. The first is my Lord and Savior, Jesus Christ. He alone is faithful and has never left me or forsaken me, ever. I cannot even begin to thank Brenda, my wife and prayer partner for the last forty years, who walked this journey with me and supported and encouraged me through it all. She continues to be my constant anchor. Added to this joy are my children: Christie and Kyle, Ashley and Ray, and Aaron and Mary, who are all enormous blessings that God has bestowed upon my life. They are wonderful young adults who have grown in their faith in Jesus and bring me joy and a crown of blessing, along with two beautiful granddaughters, Lucy and Rosalie, and our grandson Luke, who all light up my life. There is also my sister Debra and her husband Al, who was faced with the same tragedy and has come through with a steadfast faith in Jesus Christ. I can't stress enough the necessity of a church family. I want to thank my family of families, Penn Valley Church. Pastor Larry, who now is home with the Lord, but mentored me and encouraged me to give a voice to my story and to use it for ministry. To all my pastors and church elders, dear friends, and immediate family who were key in praying me through the writing of this book. I specifically did not mention names, because I know I would have left someone out. I am thankful for the countless times the Holy Spirit spoke, teaching and encouraging me through the scriptures and television ministries, preparing me for this day. All I can say is that the Lord knows all of those He used specifically for my life's journey. My hope and prayer is that you will not be without your reward. I am forever grateful and thank you from the bottom of my heart.

CHAPTER 1

My Family, My Life

I was born in a small suburban town in southeastern Pennsylvania, where my family lived in a house that my dad built. My dad literally built the first house that our family ever lived in. He was a carpenter by trade, like his father before him, along with all four of his brothers. We lived what seemed to be the middle-class lifestyle and enjoyed living close by to family. We enjoyed Sunday afternoon meals at my grandparents' house that was literally less than a mile away from our home. These Sunday meals included my uncles and aunts and cousins on my mother's side of the family. At the time, I would get to see my Great-Grandpop Palmer. These are such good memories from my childhood.

We lived in Pennsylvania until my first grade school year was complete, at which time my dad left the Alderfer family construction business that my grandfather had started for a new job in the federal government as a construction cost analyst. It was a good move for Dad in his working career, but he carried guilt with him for leaving the family business. That was because, about two weeks after Dad left the family business, my grandfather was setting trusses on a barn. Dad's brothers were working that day on the walls while Pop was inside the barn, hooking the trusses so they could be lifted in place. After many of the trusses were set, a wind kicked up, causing the collapse of all the trusses that were in place. One of those trusses that collapsed struck my grandfather, killing him. My dad told me much later, when I was in high school, that if he had only still been there working with his father, he would have been able to see that the trusses were not braced enough and could have prevented his father's death. My dad carried that guilt with him all those years, and I am sure it added to his bent to abuse alcohol. I can testify firsthand that alcohol does not change anything, but only makes it worse. Alcohol is not a solution to anything. It only gives a foothold for the enemy to destroy lives and marriages, and the children in those marriages.

It was my father's new job that took our family to Delaware, where I grew up. I repeated first grade in Delaware, which set me on a track of being one of the oldest kids in my school class at Shipley Elementary. This would prove a blessing in my high school years, which I will write about later.

So, why am I writing this book? It was not until much later that life became extremely more difficult. I really want to clarify one thing right from the start, as I share my story and my life unfolds. I believe that my father and mother loved me and always wanted what was best for me and my siblings. However, they were uncertain about how to parent as my siblings grew older and got into more difficult situations. Looking back, there was never anything said about faith or prayer. The lack of faith and prayer in our family would speak to the lack of a relationship with God, and the wisdom of God that was needed to navigate through the difficulties of life. Even the best of intentions cannot prepare us for what life sometime delivers. God uses circumstances, good and bad, to draw us unto Himself. It's just unfortunate that God gets our attention more often in tragedy rather than in triumph.

My mom was a very nurturing person at heart, much like her mother, my grandmother, whom we called Grammy. My mother and my Grammy were both loving and nurturing figures in my life. My father, on the other hand, was not that person to run to for encouragement. My father was a quiet person, not sharing too much of himself most days, but he was a great provider for his family. The only problem was, if he came home from work after stopping at the tavern, the night took a turn for the worse, especially if he did not sit down to eat dinner. Though he didn't normally have much to say, the alcohol seemed to loosen his inhibitions and he would come looking for anyone just to criticize you, tear you down. I would intentionally try and make myself scarce, but through closed doors you could hear the yelling, and I just became fearful, wondering when it was my turn. Dad would take everything out on his family, regardless of whether or not you were the cause of the difficulties of the day. I knew at a young age that this was the alcohol speaking, and not my dad. Still, it was just as terrifying, not knowing how bad it was going to get.

Both my mom and my dad are gone now, but our family tragedies that transpired were devastating, and it is that story that God has encouraged me to write and share, in the hope that it might encourage others. Not that tragedy is ever good. It's not; it tears at our hearts and even our very existence, in some cases removing all hope. But if you call out to the Lord in those moments, He will respond in His time. What the enemy meant for evil, the Lord Jesus will mean for good, according to Genesis 50:20 (NKJV), "But as for you, you meant evil against me; but God meant it for good, in order to bring it about as it is this day, to save many people alive." It has not been easy for me to recall all these memories. I have discovered that some have been suppressed for some time, and also the emotions that came with those seasons of my life. The best part has been being able to testify about how God has reached into my life and provided a way through to triumph, in spite of the tragedies.

My dad's increasing alcohol addiction was the main issue in our family. We lived and suffered through my dad's alcoholism, which led to even bigger issues in the lives of my siblings when they entered their teenage and young adult years. We were a family of six, growing up in the suburbs of Wilmington, Delaware. My oldest brother Doug was seven years older than I was. Then there was Dennis, with six years' difference between us. Dennis and Doug were only fourteen months apart in age, and being that they grew up together so close in age, they shared a bond in their relationship that I never completely understood until much later in life, because of the age difference. I shared a bedroom from time to time throughout my youth with Doug. Doug grew up as a gentle giant to me. Doug was strong and a very sensitive young man, whom I grew to love very much and looked up to. Doug was my big brother, and I was proud of that. Dennis, on the other hand, was extremely challenging as a teen. That is putting it mildly. It just seemed that wherever there was trouble, Dennis was in the middle of it. If the wrong choice could be made in any given situation, Dennis seemed to make that choice. Then there was my sister Debra. She was four years older than me, and the third child in order of birth. By the time I entered into my teenage years, Debra seemed to be busy with her own life, spending time and living away from home as much as she could. She lived this story from her own perspective and as someone who also has experienced the same shame and loss, but thankfully has a faith today that remains steadfast and strong, along with her husband Al, two adult children, and six grandchildren. This book is written from my perspective, as the youngest brother of my siblings.

Photo from 1963. Left to right, Dennis, Debra, Dale and Doug

As the youngest, I got to watch them interact with my parents, and life, in a way that only the youngest in the family could do. While I attended elementary school in Delaware, one great memory that I have is that every class had art twice a week. One art class was traditional and held in the art room. The second class was on television, and we tuned in on a TV in our homeroom. We did this from first through sixth grade. You might wonder why I am sharing about my art classes, but this is very relevant to my story, which you will see in the next chapter. The art teacher who was on TV was a very flamboyant, big-haired, beautiful lady, who for the purpose of this book I am going to refer to as "Mrs. L." Everyone in school knew who Mrs. L was. She would come and visit our classrooms maybe once a year, if we were lucky, and when she did, we all thought were looking at a television star. This woman would light up a room and just seemed to care about her students. It truly was an awesome experience, seeing and meeting Mrs. L.

My years in Delaware were accompanied by two close friends, Glenn and Ricky. These two friends were special to me. In fact, we were often referred to as "the Three Musketeers" by Ricky's mom. Glenn was a year ahead of Ricky and me. Glenn lived across the street from me. Ricky and I were in the same grade together, and he lived just one house away, behind my house. Living in the same development, only a few houses from each other, and then attending the same schools was a highlight of my life growing up in Delaware. Every year Glenn's family would take a vacation to Wildwood, NJ, and Glenn could take one friend with him—and boy, was I glad he chose me. Those times with Glenn's family provided a snapshot of a loving family and wonderful memories of being at the beach. Ricky and I shared awesome times as we went to Webster's farm together. This was a small farm that raised chickens for eggs and meat, and Mr. Webster grew pole beans and flowers to sell at his small roadside stand. We walked by this farm every day to and from elementary school. We learned a lot about chicken farming, and I even drove my first tractor on that farm. One thing that we all enjoyed together was riding our mini bikes. Well, I should clarify. Ricky and I had mini bikes. Glenn had a Honda dirt bike. We still had lots of fun together, and it became a way of coping, a way of forgetting the hard things going on in my family as things continued to spiral out of control.

We lived in a day and age when we could go outside and play all day, just about anywhere in the neighborhood. The boundaries of the neighborhood were limitless, at least for me. There was just one stipulation in that I must be home for dinner. Dinnertime grew increasingly stressful for the Alderfer household. This time should be a peaceful time where everyone can share about their day and eat in a relaxed atmosphere, like I had seen and experienced at Glenn's house. That was not the case for most evening meals in my home.

As I already stated, the tone of the evening was dictated by the type and amount of alcohol my dad had consumed before returning home from his day's work. Dad sat at the head of the table, and Doug sat at the other end. I sat to Dad's right, and Dennis was next to me. By the time I got to be ten and eleven years old, Dennis was well into his teens, and the trouble he was getting himself into had become increasingly more serious. The difficulties were no longer isolated to school, but extended outside of school and often escalated to the point that the county police and even state police became involved, frequently showing up at our house. I was extremely embarrassed by this. I was the only kid on the block who had the police coming to my home. What was wrong with my family? I felt shame. Well, my dad's attention to these issues seemed to come out during mealtime. Once the topic of my brother's behavior was brought up, it did not take long for my father to react. He would often reach over me to get to my brother Dennis. There was chaos most evenings at our home. I learned to cope at the dinner table by eating fast and then excusing myself from the table. I would then straight-arm the front door to get outside to play with my friends.

I remember one evening sitting down to a meal. My mom had made chicken parmesan. She would serve our dinner to us with a chicken patty on top of spaghetti, covered with lots of sauce. Before we were even able to start the meal, Dad addressed an issue about school with Dennis. Dennis got so mad, he grabbed his plate of food and slammed it upside down on the kitchen table as hard as he could, breaking the plate and splattering his food all over the walls and ceiling in the kitchen. My dad instantly reached over me and pulled Dennis toward him in a full-out brawl, with me underneath them. As the room cleared, I found myself in tears along with my sister, both of us devastated from the event that had just happened. It was Debra and me that spent the rest of the evening cleaning up what Dennis had done. This really will become a metaphor for future events.

The fear of what was going to happen next, and how bad it was going to get, gripped me every night as a young man. Through this time my parents had more and more trouble coping. Dad's stress increased not only at home, but at work as well. He dealt with the stress by drinking more and more alcohol. If my father came in the door and sat down at the dinner table to eat, it was going to be an okay evening. But if my dad walked in the door after stopping for a drink and bringing a six-pack home—or worse, a bottle of whiskey—and then skipping dinner, we were going to be in for a rough evening. I lived every day in that tension, not knowing how bad the arguing and fighting was going to be. Needless to say, this type of situation is not healthy or stable for anyone to grow up in, and this held true for all of us in our home. When Dad was sober, he would not express anything, good or bad. He was a strangely quiet man. The alcohol freed my dad to express his feelings that he could not share when sober. This kept us all in a form of bondage to fear. I watched my dad be very hard on my older siblings. Under the influence of alcohol, my dad had the ability to criticize and to be extremely demeaning. The target was not so much me, but I observed it as it played out in the lives of my siblings. All I tried to do as the youngest was to be a peacemaker. I would do anything I could to keep peace in the house.

Something was broken in my family, and I did not know what it was. I did not see this played out in my friends' families. This was pretty much how life was for me. I was living on edge, not knowing what was going to happen next. Mom and Dad did take us to church every now and then, but we really never had any kind of spiritual upbringing other than the occasional church service. You know, Christmas and Easter. There was one Sunday after the church service when my parents went to the pastor and had me baptized. Nothing was said to me other than the fact that I was to stand by this baptismal bowl, and as the pastor prayed, he sprinkled water on my head. I knew that I was baptized, but I did not understand why. At the very best, I had a spiritual awareness that there must be something more, something greater, but still did not understand what this might be. By this time I was approaching junior high and really wondering what life was all about.

CHAPTER 2

A Cry Out to God

All the yelling went on in our home what felt like almost every evening. Whether it was between my dad and my brothers or between my brothers, it seemed like the atmosphere of our home caused me to live in fear, which caused anxiety. I never knew what was going to happen or when it was going to happen. Whatever it was, I knew it was not going to be good. That was my experience at home. The worst was when I would lie in bed at night and be woken up to yelling and hearing doors slam, sometimes along with actual physical fighting going on right outside my bedroom door. My life had become very difficult emotionally, and I did not know what or where to turn for help. I would walk into my mom's bedroom only to find her in tears, crying over something that had happened. I would ask her what was wrong, and her answer every time was, "Nothing." Well, I knew enough to know that that wasn't true. There was something drastically wrong in my family.

I was also embarrassed, because my friends' families were not experiencing the same issues. When the police drove into our development I just knew they were coming to my house, and I was right. Then one day, something happened within our family which brought me to a new level of hopelessness. I retreated to my bedroom one afternoon, feeling defeated. I do not remember to this day what exactly had happened to bring me to this point, but I was feeling that I just could not go on any longer, feeling hopeless, and tired of the fear and uncertainty of how bad it was going to get. I closed the door to my bedroom sat down on my bed and cried, wondering why I was even here. What was life all about? Why was I ever born? My life was broken, and I remember the thought going through my mind that I didn't want to live anymore. There had to be more to life than what I was experiencing. The hopelessness brought me to the point that, at the age of thirteen, I was thinking of ending my own life. I even went into my closet and took my shotgun out of the gun case and leaned it in the corner by the closet door. As I sat in my room looking at the shotgun, I remembered that we had an old, black Bible that was in the hallway bookshelf. I went to get the Bible, and I brought it back into my room and closed the door. As I opened it up and looked through the many pages, stopping to read and trying to understand what life was all about, it only added to my

TRAGEDY AND TRIUMP: FIND HIM FAITHFUL

confusion. I was looking for hope and the answer to my problems, but I could not understand anything that I was reading. Out of the agony of my life, with a broken spirit, hopeless and not wanting to live, holding that Bible in my hands, I cried out to a God I did not know, *"God, if You're real, You have to reveal Yourself to me! Because I do not want to live life like this anymore!"* There was nothing but silence after that cry of my heart, but looking back at the shotgun, I determined I would give God a chance to respond. With that, I got up, put my shotgun away, and placed the Bible back on the bookshelf in the hallway, and I ran outside to find my friends—a very welcome distraction.

What was to happen next was an answer to that prayer, offered up in desperate haste. It was within the next week, when I was at school, that God did reach out to me through some friends. One day right after choir practice, I got up from my seat and looked across the auditorium. I saw a group of kids talking together. I knew each of the kids individually, but I had never seen them talking together as a group before. It made me curious, so I made my way over to them and included myself in their conversation, and they gladly welcomed me. I asked them what they were talking about. They responded that they were discussing what they were planning to do at youth group this week, and that I ought to come. These kids had no idea what I had just prayed in my room a few days before. I looked at this as an opportunity to discover what this youth group was all about and wondered if this could be God, reaching back to me in an answer to my desperate plea. Of course I responded with yes. I wanted to go! When I went home that very day, I asked Doug if he would please take me over to Chester Bethel United Methodist Church so I could attend youth group. Doug not only took me to youth group on Wednesday evenings, he also took me over on Sunday mornings and made sure I had a ride.

One of the girls in the group's father was the pastor of the church, and her mother was the Sunday school teacher and youth group leader. She was such a kind person and was now my Sunday school teacher. I think it was my second time attending Sunday school, Mrs. L was teaching on Romans 6:23 (NKJV), "For the wages of sin is death, but the gift of God is eternal life in Christ Jesus our Lord." She explained that our sins do earn a wage, and that wage is eternal separation from God; however, she went on to say that God has a gift for us—all of us. At this point, I thought she was talking directly to me. It was like I was the only person in the room. Mrs. L was holding a Bible in her hand. She extended her arms out in front of her, towards me, as if the gift was just for me, and said, "If I have a gift for you, I will say that this gift is just for you, and I even put your name on it." Then she asked the question,

"But when is that gift really yours?" Mrs. L said, "It's not yours until you reach out and take it!" Well, I reached out and took that gift that day! I prayed to ask Jesus to forgive my sins, and to come into my life and be my Lord and Savior that Sunday morning! That was March 25, 1973. I remember that date, because right after she finished praying with us and class was over, I went up to her and told her that I had prayed along with her. She smiled and asked me if I had my own Bible. I responded no. The Bible that she was using as an object lesson that morning, she opened it up to the front cover and wrote my name inside: Dale Alderfer from Chester Bethel United Methodist Church, March 25, 1973. That was the day I became a new creation in Christ Jesus. Now that my eyes were open to a new relationship with Jesus Christ, it started me on a new journey.

Now, I am not sure if you made the connection. Mrs. L, the pastor's wife who shared the gospel that Sunday morning and then prayed with me to receive Jesus as Savior, was the same flamboyant, big-haired, kind woman who had taught art class on TV in my entire elementary school years. The Lord used her to lovingly lead me to Himself and give me my first Bible. That was always very special to me. I enjoyed getting to know Mrs. L. She was a very loving person. Several times she had me over to her house after church for lunch with the family, where she would do nothing but love and encourage me. I feel she had an impression that things were not so good in my home. But I was so glad that the God of the Bible did respond to my desperate cry for Him to reveal Himself to me, and He responded with the kids in a youth group and used an art teacher and pastor's wife to change my life through the good news of the Gospel of Christ.

I was excited about my newfound faith and realized that what I had just found was the solution for my family, and this set me on a course to pray for Jesus to intervene in my family. I prayed for their salvation, knowing that what had happened inside me was the solution for them as well. I prayed for God to change them and save them from their sins, and to change their hearts and lives. I would've liked to tell you at this point that everything was made right, and everything went on to have a storybook ending, and we lived happily ever after. I can assure you, that was not the case.

CHAPTER 3

Troubles Continue

My brother Dennis continued to get into trouble. At this point it wasn't notes from the school principal that came home; it was the state police and county police showing up at our door regularly, at all hours of the night, looking for Dennis. Dennis was getting into drugs, and at one point he came running in the door at home hollering for help from Dad and Doug. He said that this carload of guys had followed him home and were going to kill him. My brother and my father responded by running out the door to chase away the carload of thugs that were coming after Dennis. It was like this night after night, me feeling powerless to change anything and wondering if God was going to show up in an answer to my prayers and change my circumstances.

We would travel back to Pennsylvania some weekends to visit my grandfather. Grammy had passed away from cancer at this point, and Pop was lonely living in a big house all by himself. He was asking if we would be willing to move back to Pennsylvania and into his house with him. One weekend I chose to stay at home in Delaware while Mom, Dad, and Doug chose to go to PA. That weekend was an eye-opener for me. I saw just how far Dennis had gotten involved into the drug scene. As soon as my parents left the house, Dennis came home with several friends. They just took over the house and started dealing drugs from our home phone. There were several different bags of amphetamines and barbiturates on the kitchen table, along with marijuana, and lots and lots of alcohol. The house became a scary place for me to be. I did not know who was going to come through the door of my home next. I told Dennis he should not be doing this; however, it fell on deaf ears. Thankfully I was able to retreat to Glenn's house, where I slept overnight just so I did not have to be part of that scene.

Dennis was continually in and out of trouble with the law and went into rehab several times, only to return to the drugs. One of the times he returned from rehab he was determined to stay off the drugs. I told him that he needed to flush the marijuana that he had stashed behind his stereo speaker cover. We went to the basement, where he took the baggie full of dope and with my encouragement, I watched him flush it all down the toilet. I was hopeful that he was serious this time with his recovery, and I continued to pray for his deliverance from the drugs.

It had been a little over one year since I had come to Christ as Savior when my father's job got transferred back to Philadelphia, and my parents decided to move back to Pennsylvania where we would be living with my grandfather, my mother's father. I was excited and sad at the same time, because it was going to take me away from my church and all of my youth group friends that had supported and encouraged me in my relationship with Christ. At this point, I felt really alone. I was in a new school without my closest friends and the youth group to support me. It was then that I found a television ministry called "In Touch," by Dr. Charles Stanley. The Lord used In Touch Ministries to feed and nourish my soul. I am still thankful to this day for Dr. Charles Stanley and his faithful teaching from the Word of God.

I continued to pray for my family, however, with little hope for the change that our family desperately needed. For six years I sought the Lord and prayed for the salvation of my family members. As a young Christian, and with limited mentoring and discipleship to seek help from, I start to develop some wrong theology. After seeing no improvement in my circumstances at home with my family, I began to think that God would never answer my prayers for my family. During this time of praying for my family Dennis spiraled downhill, which added additional stress and added to my dad's need to cope. His main coping mechanism was alcohol, and when drinking he made the entire situation a lot more stressful. Dennis, in hopes of changing and getting himself straightened out, signed up for the Navy. His drug and alcohol addictions were not getting better, and he thought the Navy would provide a clean break.

Dennis completed basic training at the naval station in Great Lakes, Illinois. As a family we drove out to his basic training graduation in hopes of showing our family's support for his newfound success in the Navy. Dennis had lost a lot of weight and was in the best shape of his recent life. I came away from that trip more hopeful than ever for Dennis and our family. That feeling was short-lived, because within the first month of Dennis graduating, we received a phone call that Dennis was in the hospital. Apparently Dennis went on a drug and alcohol binge and was considered AWOL by the Navy. Upon returning to the base he was arrested and placed in handcuffs. Dennis was always good with hurtful words and somehow behaved disrespectfully, saying something that angered the MPs, leading them to beat him while he was handcuffed and in custody. We only received this information because the Navy had to explain why Dennis was so badly injured, requiring him to be hospitalized. My parents were told that the bones were shattered on the entire side of his face. It was going to take some time for those injuries to heal, but once

Dennis was well enough physically, he was then sent to the mental ward for psychiatric evaluation. Our family was told that Dennis' injuries had triggered schizophrenia, and that he was now being treated for it. It was not long before he was transferred from Illinois to the VA hospital in Coatesville, Pennsylvania. This hospital was an hour from our home, and I would drive my mom to visit with him. Dad never went to see Dennis.

Not much later, the Navy informed us on Dennis' behalf that he was going to be honorably discharged from the Navy and would be given $950 a month for disability. It was at that time that my parents questioned further as to what had exactly happened to Dennis, and as far as I know we never received a straight answer from that time forward from the Navy. It seemed awfully funny that Dennis had broken military law, and now he was being honorably discharged, and in addition he was going to be receiving disability. I watched this drama with Dennis take a toll on my parents personally, as well as on their marriage. Once Dennis was released from the VA hospital in Coatesville, he came back home to live. Then our lives and conditions began to worsen. Dennis was acting irrational, sleeping most of the day, and up all night when everyone else was trying to get rest. One of the most eerie things you can witness is to observe someone dealing with multiple personalities. I had the opportunity to see all sides of those personalities.

This was an extremely stressful time for me, not knowing what was going to happen next, but I continued to pray for my God to intervene and heal and make all things right. At this time my faith did become weary, but I always held out hope for a better outcome. By this time I was a senior in high school. I did not have many friends since leaving my youth group behind in Delaware, but one day I was standing outside my homeroom, waiting for class to start, and I saw this girl walk out of the homeroom next door. She was captivating and beautiful. I had never seen or noticed this girl at high school before. I was wondering how I had missed seeing her during my sophomore and junior years. As she walked by, I said to my homeroom teacher, Mr. Cell, that I had to get to meet this girl. He just looked at me and chuckled, "Yeah, right." I inquired about her from everyone I knew and found out she was the captain of the majorettes in the high school band. I found myself trying to position myself to get to meet her. She had captivated my eyes and my heart, and her name was Brenda. I was able to work up the nerve to ask Brenda out and she actually said yes, only for me to find out later that she only said yes to our date because she had never been to a concert at the spectrum in Philly before. I wasn't deterred by her hard-to-get attitude; I just wanted to get to know her.

Brenda was a breath of fresh air brought into my life. I discovered that we both had situations at home that we were seeking the Lord's help for and were pleading for Him to intervene on behalf of our families. Brenda had just recently lost her dad to cancer. Her family was also struggling to make ends meet and to overcome the loss of her father. She certainly did not have it easy at that time in her life either. It was because of Brenda that I was able to find my way back to church. Brenda attended church at Montgomery Baptist, where she had gone since she was a little girl. The Lord brought Brenda not only into my life, but into my heart as well, and just at the right time. I needed her intervention, especially at this season of my life, and she was a true blessing from the Lord. Brenda and I prayed together for our families. She gave me hope and encouragement, and I would like to think I blessed her when she needed encouragement. We attended church each week. The pastor of Brenda's church had started a discipleship group and asked me to be a part of that group, and I began to grow in the Word and in my faith. This short season was a blessing, and I was so thankful for the Son to shine through the clouds of my heart. To this very day, Brenda is the brightest blessing in my life! This was all in preparation for the tragedy that was headed towards my family.

Dennis was not responding to any treatment or medications, and there was no improvement in his schizophrenia. Most of the time Dennis would not take his medication, either, and you could see it reflected in his personality. Because of this, Dennis was not able to live on his own. Dennis' inability to live on his own was emphasized one day. Without notifying anyone, Dennis left home. Unknown to us, Dennis had bought a car and driven across the country. He was gone for a few months when my parents received a phone call from a mental health hospital in Utah, where he had been admitted for his strange behavior. After many days of treatment, my parents eventually paid to fly Dennis home and seek further treatment at a VA hospital closer to home. My parents also did not know that while Dennis was making his way west, he had purchased a 1977 AMC Gremlin and a new Les Paul guitar. They did not know this until they received a phone call from a gas station owner in Utah who said they had this car registered to Dennis, and all his personal belongings were locked in the car. My parents made the arrangements with the gas station owner for an individual who needed to come east and was willing to drive the car back to PA. My parents paid for the car to be driven back to PA, along with Dennis' belongings.

Now every night at home was nerve-racking, not knowing what was going to happen. Dennis' behavior was increasingly hard to deal with. Doug, Mom, and I spent an entire night sitting by Dennis' bed. I was praying over him and telling Dennis that Jesus could help him. I had never witnessed demon possession before this night. I am positive that what my mother, brother, and I witnessed throughout the night was Dennis being tormented by demons. I was never so scared, confused, and drained emotionally as I was that night. I prayed and prayed over Dennis as he screamed out. He would yell at the top of his lungs that the devil was getting him and his body, and face would contort in agony. After that night, I found myself spending as much time as I could out of the house. I would work extra hours or spend all my time at Brenda's house. I would do anything, just as long as I did not have to be around the situation at home.

Brenda and I grew closer and closer in spite of my family's ongoing difficulties. We were in a committed relationship and sought Jesus together. It was on Christmas Eve, 1977, after we attended a Christmas Eve church service, that I asked Brenda to marry me. She said yes! I had not been this happy in a long time. I was certainly having the mountaintop experience of my life! God was blessing me beyond what I could ever imagine with my engagement to Brenda. All of this joy unfolded with me not knowing that in just six days, I would be asked to endure tragedy that would change everything in my family.

I don't know how anyone could be prepared to endure what happened on December 30, 1977. I certainly was not. I was working in the basement at home, and I heard a loud discussion break out upstairs in the kitchen. These loud discussions and arguments happened a lot of times, and I would do my best to stay away or out of them, so I listened from the basement. It turned out that Dennis had received a check for $9,000 for back pay from the Navy. My mom and dad were attempting to tell Dennis that he needed to save this money and go to a trade school, and not just blow the money. Dennis was not having it; this was "his" money, and he wanted to spend it on what he wanted to spend it on. The discussion turned into a full-out argument over the use of this money. As I was in the basement working on a project, I could overhear everything going on right above me. I stayed in the basement until I heard the argument stop. The arguing only stopped when Dad left the house to deposit the check into Dennis' bank account. The bank was only about ten minutes away, but in those ten minutes, our family's world was turned upside down. Once the arguing had ceased, I figured it was a good time to make my escape, so I headed upstairs.

CHAPTER 4

Tragedy

As I came up from the basement into the kitchen, my mom was alone, at the sink washing the dishes. Dennis was no longer in the kitchen, and Dad was headed to the bank. As I was walking by my mom, I mentioned that I was going to go up and get changed and then pick Brenda up, and we were going to her work's Christmas party. I continued past my mom and started up the stairs to the second floor. As I reached the top of the stairs and turned to go to my room, I could see that my parents' bedroom door was slightly open. Through the crack I saw my father's rifle gun case on the bed. I stopped and walked over to the door and slowly pushed the door open to reveal Dennis, holding my dad's hunting rifle waist-high and pointing it in my direction. I said, "Denny, what are you doing!" in a firm voice, and what happened next seemed to happen in slow motion, but I know it played out in a matter of minutes. I had thought that I caught Dennis with the rifle *before* he'd had an opportunity to load it. So I walked toward him with my hand reaching for the muzzle of the rifle. Dennis began to shake and was backing up, pleading with me not to come any closer. I stopped at this point and backed up to the doorway into the bedroom. Unbeknownst to me at that moment, my mom had heard what I had said to my brother, "Denny, what are you doing!" and she had started up the stairs toward the commotion. Dennis had walked forward toward me, with the rifle still waist-high and directed at me, and when my mother crested the top of the steps, Dennis turned the rifle toward her and pulled the trigger. The rifle went off and the bullet traveled between me and the door jamb, striking my mother in her upper right shoulder area, knocking her backwards. She collapsed and tumbled down the steep wooden steps.

Dennis, at that moment, was ejecting the shell to load another round, and I wanted to jump on him with all that was in me and tackle him and take the rifle away—but just as I was lunging forward, something or someone, an unseen force, strongly gripped my shoulders from behind and pulled me backwards, to the point of being so far off balance that I had to step back to stay on my feet. That same force turned me completely around so that I was looking at my mother at the bottom of the steps. I instantly hurried down the steps and proceeded to pick my mom up, because I did not know what Dennis was going to do next. Was he going to start shooting down the stairs? I did not know. As I was carrying my mother out of the line of fire, I looked up the stairs and I saw my grandfather walk out into the hallway. My grandfather had been lying down in his room taking a nap when he was startled awake by the gunshot. Not knowing that his only daughter had just been shot, Pop was trying to figure out what had just happened. I had no idea what Denny might do next, so I yelled up the stairs, *"Pop, Denny has a gun!"* I continued on to the opposite side of the living room, away from Dennis' sight line.

As I laid my mom down, it was then that another shot rang out. My heart sank, thinking that Dennis had shot my grandfather too. After laying my mom on the floor, I ran back upstairs to find my grandfather leaning over Dennis' body. Dennis had turned the gun under his chin and taken his own life. You could clearly see there was no way Dennis was alive at that point, and my attention turned immediately back to my mother. I told Pop that Denny had shot Mom, and she was downstairs. I grabbed the dish towels to address the bleeding on Mom, and Pop grabbed the phone and called the police. The police responded, coming through the front and back doors simultaneously, with guns drawn. I yelled to the officer coming in the front door of the home that my brother had shot my mom, and then shot himself. The officer came over to me to assess the situation and told me to stay and keep pressure on the gunshot wound. The officer then went upstairs to confirm what I had said. When the EMTs showed up and took over my mom's care, the police instantly pulled me into the kitchen, separating me from my grandfather. There was no time to reflect on what had just happened.

This all took place within the time it took my dad to go to the bank and return back home. It was when the ambulance arrived that my dad walked back into the house to this horrific scene after depositing Denny's check. Dad was able to travel in the ambulance with Mom, who by the way had never lost consciousness all this time. The police questioned me in the kitchen. They asked me to explain exactly what had happened. They did the same to my grandfather out in the living room. At one point, the police asked me to show them exactly where I was standing and took me upstairs, where Dennis's lifeless body lay on the floor. The bedroom was a mess from the suicide. Blood was splattered everywhere. The police had me go over to where I was positioned and where Dennis was positioned before and during the shooting. I know this was necessary as part of the police investigation; however, the tragedy that just taken place was sinking in, and I was only beginning to feel the effects of what would be part of my life's story forever. With Dennis still lying on the floor, I felt I could not stay in the bedroom, and in a panic I ran out to get away from the horrific scene. It was then that the police asked me if I was willing to go to the police station. I acknowledged yes, and the detectives loaded me in the back of their police car and drove me down to the station.

While at the police station I was introduced to the county coroner, who again asked me to tell what had happened and this time recorded my statement. After what seemed like a few hours I was allowed to leave, and I returned home. I still did not know very much about the condition of my mother, other than that she was airlifted down to Jefferson Hospital in Philadelphia, and was placed in intensive care. After being released from the police station and returning home, to say that I was walking back into a total mess is vastly an understatement. Since my dad was with my mom at the hospital, I put my attention at home, where I was faced with cleaning up the aftermath of Dennis' suicide. It looked like the set of a horror movie, only for me this was real life. There was blood and other remains everywhere. It was like my body was moving, but I wasn't there. It was surreal. I had to come to grips with the fact that this had really happened. The smell; I will never forget that smell. To have to clean the remains of my own brother off the walls, doors, and ceiling was just something I can't and won't forget. I will be forever grateful for those who helped to clean up.

I had not seen my older brother Doug until this point. Doug had returned home to find this same horrific scene. Doug now had to face the reality that his younger brother Dennis had actually done this to our mother, and now Dennis was dead. Doug did not say much, but went to work on the cleanup. Unfortunately, I found out much later that this tragedy affected Doug more than he was able to express at the time, and he would struggle with the devastation from the attempted murder and suicide. Our whole family was deeply affected, but it may have affected Doug more because Doug and Dennis had grown up together so close in age. They shared a connection that I could not, because of birth order. It was now, more than ever, that I was so thankful for my uncles and cousins on my mom's side of the family. Many were volunteer firefighters and had a heart for service. They showed up more than willing to assist us in this devastating cleanup. It is my prayer that God will provide extended blessings to their account because of this selfless act of kindness, shown through their service to us.

You're probably wondering about an update on my mom. She was stabilized but still in critical condition at Jefferson Hospital, in the ICU. Brenda and I made the trip to Philly as often as we could. Her most serious injuries were to her lungs. When Mom fell down the stairs she had broken multiple ribs, puncturing both lungs. You can only imagine the guilt that I carried, thinking I had added to her injuries by picking her up and carrying her out of the line of fire. Her right collarbone had two inches missing as a result of the gunshot. It was necessary to place a metal plate to bridge the gap of the missing bone. My mom was in intensive care for the next six weeks, and we were only able to see her for fifteen minutes every two hours. We prayed for healing, physically and emotionally.

We did not know how much Mom knew about Dennis, as she was unable to communicate due to being placed on a ventilator and floating in and out of consciousness while in the ICU. So, we waited to bring it up until we knew she would be able to process it. When Mom finally could ask about Dennis, we told her that Dennis was dead. Her response was one of relief. I do not think this was a selfish relief or a vindictive relief, but a relief that her son who had battled demons all of his teenage and adult life was not going to face further condemnation or jail, allowing the despair to continue along with the heartache. I really believe that afternoon, when Dennis fired that shot striking my mother, it was a depth of sin and depravity that crossed the line for the Lord. I also believe that the presence that stopped me from disarming my brother was an angel of the Lord, and the Lord did not want me to stop what was about to happen. I have asked God why many times. I always run to the truth of His Word, the Bible, and in Romans 1:28-32 (NKJV) it says, "And even as they did not like to retain God in their knowledge, God gave them over to a debased mind, to do those things which are not fitting; being filled with all unrighteousness, sexual immorality, wickedness, covetousness, maliciousness; full of envy, murder, strife, deceit, evil-mindedness; they are whisperers, backbiters, haters of God, violent, proud, boasters, inventors of evil things, disobedient to parents, undiscerning, untrustworthy, unloving, unforgiving, unmerciful; who, knowing the righteous judgment of God, that those who practice such things are deserving of death, not only do the same but also approve of those who practice them."

In something as horrible as this, God was there! God does not cause us to walk in darkness and sin. Dennis chose to deny God and reject His love and forgiveness, and in the rejection of God he chose a destructive path. I do believe that if my father had returned from the bank and Dennis still had the rifle, he may have attempted to murder him too. I believe I can say with a level of certainty and authority from God's Word, the Bible, that what stopped Dennis from pulling the trigger when the muzzle of the rifle was only three feet from my stomach was that God had placed His hand of protection over me at that moment in time. I certainly could not testify to that while in the heat of the situation, but looking back, I can now see that Jesus was at work, protecting me. God's providential hand was also at work on my behalf when, after I witnessed the attempted murder of my mother, my grandfather witnessed Dennis' suicide. The police instantly separated my grandfather and me, and when our testimony of this attempted murder and suicide came together, the truth brought no doubt to their investigation. I am sure this could have been very different if there were questions in the investigation. But God had this also in the palm of His hand, which brought a swift closure to the investigation. I can't help but see God's hand in this, allowing closure to this murder-suicide investigation. As I mentioned, my brother Doug, who had returned home to find this devastation on December 30, was forever changed emotionally, and I believe he never really recovered from it.

CHAPTER 5

Tragedy Strikes Again

I remember Doug would not talk to me while we were cleaning up the bedroom after Dennis' suicide. I would look over at him and could see him fighting through the heartache and sadness over what had just transpired. After this, Doug became more socially reserved. Doug would go out of his way not to have to interact with people. He would return home from a day out working and obsess about someone who he thought was staring at him. Doug was in the grips of a tailspin in his life, certainly aided by what he had experienced and internalized from the tragedy. This was something that broke my heart, because Doug was a gentle-spirited man. He was someone who wanted to help everyone and would not ever desire to hurt anyone. Remember, it was Doug who made sure that I made it to youth group and church. Doug was a kind person and an even better big brother to me.

Doug was a believer in Jesus, and we would encourage each other in our faith in spite of the very real struggles of everyday life. Doug lived at home until 1982, at which time my parents thought it was time for him to move out. Doug was still socially reserved and did not attend church, but would watch church on TV. After moving to his own apartment not too far from home, he seemed to have landed on his feet. Doug was self-employed, and in the early 80s the economy was recovering from the late 70s recession from the Jimmy Carter era. He had met a young lady whom he was getting serious with. But unknown to me at the time, Doug had run up credit card debt to run his business, and he financed his living expenses with that same credit card. His relationship began to fail, and the home improvement business was floundering. The extensive credit card debt was catching up to him. Doug slipped into a depression. This depression did not go unnoticed by Brenda and me. Brenda and I married in July of 1980, and Doug would come to the house from time to time to visit and to help me with my fixer-up projects that were always ongoing with an old house. We encouraged Doug and prayed with him and for him to recover from his current circumstances.

I noticed that his depression had progressed and was slipping even deeper into sadness when he stopped at our house one day. After Dennis' death, my dad seemed to be even harder on Doug. Because Doug was in the building trade and that was my dad's specialty and background, it seemed like whatever Doug did was not good enough. When Doug was helping me with building my garage, Dad would stop and just point out and criticize how Doug was doing it wrong. It's not that Doug was doing it wrong; he just was not doing it the way my dad would, which made it wrong in my dad's opinion. To this day I feel badly, because I would say to Doug, "Let's just do it Dad's way, just to keep the peace, and move on." Sorry, Doug! This did not help Doug, and I now think this may have added to his depressed state. Doug even turned to alcohol himself, and as a result wrecked a brand-new pickup truck, which also resulted in him receiving a DUI charge. Doug's emotional state and life circumstances had gotten the best of him, and as a result he attempted to take his own life by slitting his wrists. He was sent to the hospital, where his physical injuries were addressed, and then sent to a mental health hospital to deal with his emotional illnesses.

I walked with Doug through these seasons of his life, visiting him at the hospital, and eventually attending DUI classes with him so he would be able to obtain his driving privileges again. Doug did bounce back for a short season, only find himself slipping back into depression. Again we prayed with Doug about his life, asking the Lord to provide a way for him out of his current circumstances. Doug stopped coming to the house, and I became concerned. Brenda and I were out one afternoon not far from Doug's apartment. Brenda turned to me, and I could see in her eyes that she was thinking the same thing I was, that we needed to stop and see Doug. Doug was home and very reserved during our visit. I could just feel the oppression and depression in Doug's apartment. We talked and encouraged him and prayed again. I spoke specifically that our God is a God of second, third, fourth... really, as many chances we need. If we fall short in any area of our lives, 1 John 1:9 (NKJV) says, "If we confess our sins, He is faithful and just to forgive us our sins and to cleanse us from all unrighteousness." When we know Jesus as Lord, we can pray 1 John 1:9 *not* to be forgiven, but *because* we are forgiven. The focus is on God's amazing grace and love breaking the bond of condemnation. The Bible points out in Romans 2:4 that it is the goodness of God that leads us to repentance. We left Doug that day, asking God to bring health and to restore the joy of his salvation back to Doug's life.

What happened next, I was not prepared for. I was at work in early April, 1983, and my supervisor came to me very solemnly, telling me that I had a personal phone call from my mother. I swallowed hard because of my supervisor's face, and the fact we did not receive calls at work unless it was an emergency. I followed Joe to his office. My mother told me that Doug had taken his own life, and that the local police department needed a family member to come to the police station. My heart sank to the depths of despair. I went to the police department to answer questions about Doug and to provide current information for Doug. Doug had died as a result of a self-inflicted gunshot wound to his head. Before leaving the police station, I made plans for Doug's body to be picked up by a local funeral home. My parents were totally unable to respond to this situation, so I took the responsibility of planning Doug's funeral. I also had the responsibility of meeting the landlady of Doug's apartment the very next morning to address cleanup, and the removal of Doug's personal belongings.

You can imagine my hesitancy when it came to seeing the apartment and the suicide cleanup. I had been through one cleanup that was horrific, and now I was facing this second cleanup task by myself. The next morning when I was preparing to go to the apartment to meet the landlady, I noticed a pickup truck pulling into my driveway, first thing in the morning. I walked out of the house to be greeted by a dear friend, Fred, from work. I asked Fred, "Why are you here?" He told me he had taken the day off of work and was there to help me with the apartment cleanup and cleanout. Wow. I had not told anyone that this was going to happen, but the Lord sent me an angel with the name of

Fred that day, for which I will be eternally grateful, and he will always hold a special place in my heart and my story.

On the day of Doug's funeral, I drove my parents' car to the funeral home to park it in preparation for the funeral. The funeral home was on the next block from Pop's home. When I parked the car at the funeral home, Phil, the funeral director, came out of the funeral home, approached me, and said that he thought it was important that someone in the family view the body before the funeral. You see, the funeral was going to be a closed casket because of the gunshot wound. I took a deep breath as we walked toward the funeral parlor. Phil opened the casket, and there my brother was, looking so peaceful. Phil had prepared Doug's body so it could have had an open casket. Seeing Doug brought an overwhelming sense of peace to my own heart. I just cannot explain how seeing Doug brought peace. My only regret is that I did not go and get my mother and father and insist that they have a private viewing, hoping it to be a powerful time that would bring some peace and closure to such a violent and devastating circumstance. The entire time during the funeral service I could feel the Lord holding me up. Somehow, I was immersed in His peace when everyone else was overwhelmed by Doug's passing and heartbroken for my family with not just one, but now two suicides.

I remember, when the service was over, walking out of the funeral home to get in the car to go to the graveside, and it felt as if my feet were not touching the ground as I was walking. It felt so real that I purposely stopped and looked down at my feet. I can picture exactly where that spot is to this day. As I looked up, I was smiling, knowing that the Lord was lifting me. I looked over and saw my great aunt looking at me with a facial expression like, "What are you smiling about?" That was a surreal moment in my tragedy, when what I believe to be God sent His ministering angels to my aid, to hold me up when I needed it most.

As expected, my mom and dad were devastated at the loss of their two sons. They spent very little time together, and as far as I know, they never really talked in depth to each other about Dennis and Doug and their feelings. But you could see that my mom was depressed most days. Mom did attend counseling for her grief and depression, and at the request of the counselor, I attended with her for support. She carried guilt more than anything. I loved my mother, and I know she loved her family, even though our family was torn and hurt by the aftermath of the tragedies from my brothers' suicides. Not only did my mother carry the emotional damage to her last day, she carried the physical damage with her as a result of the gunshot. She supported her right arm by cradling it in her left arm. She was in pain twenty-four hours per day, along with the fact that this devastating injury came at the hands of her own child, whom she had given birth to! The doctors could not provide the pain relief she needed, so she turned to the numbing effects of alcohol. Mom was able to hide her drinking much better than my father.

I would describe my family's existence as surviving, not thriving. Brenda and I continued to pray for them and come alongside them whenever we had the opportunity to do so. Life did go on. I had to work to pay the bills, and my family was growing. We celebrated the births of Christie and Ashley, but also mourned the loss of my dear grandfather soon after the birth of our second daughter. Two years later, my dear mother passed away from liver disease, in 1990. My father immediately prepped the house for sale—anxious to leave the home, with all the past horror and devastation, behind. He would have done this while my mother was still alive, but she refused to sell the house, not wanting to leave the home she had grown up in. Dad had purchased the building lot next door to me and went ahead and had a house built next door to Brenda and me. After the house was completed Dad moved next door to us in 1992, and this ended up being the best time that I had with my father. Dad was dealing with a heart issue and ending up suffering a heart attack that required a quadruple bypass. It was after this that the doctors told

Dad he had to quit smoking and drinking, or it would eventually kill him. This must have been enough motivation, because Dad stopped drinking and smoking from that time on. Now that Dad was off the alcohol he was a totally different person, and these ended up being the best years that I spent with my father. Brenda and I had a third child, Aaron, whom my dad really got a kick out of, being that he lived so close. Of course, he loved all his grandchildren.

Then in 1995 Dad developed an arterial cancer. After they removed eighty percent of the tumor through surgery, Dad was given radiation in hopes of shrinking the balance of the tumor. Through this time, Brenda and I would take Dad to appointments. Dad was a quiet man and really did not speak of spiritual things. I would continue to share and encourage him. He was doing well in the summer of 1995, taking natural remedies, and was even playing golf once a week. It was not until that November that Dad had a tumor bleed which required another operation to stop the bleeding. This surgery taxed Dad's body, and in December he returned to the hospital because he had experienced a mild heart attack. His body just was not holding up under the resurgence of the cancer and his heart issues. In the spiraling down of my father's health I felt an urgency to settle Dad's eternal destiny. I went to the hospital that day with my Bible in hand and with prepared scriptures to read. As

I read the scriptures to Dad, I stopped and asked him if he had ever accepted Christ as Savior. He responded to me abruptly, "Why are you always talking about this?" I responded, "You are here with me now, and I can talk to you. After you're gone I can no longer talk to you, and I want to know if you're going to heaven." He again abruptly replied, "I took care of that a long time ago." That is all the confession of faith I received from my dad, because he died in February, 1996. I lived a long time after Dad's death with the enemy torturing me with what I thought was my dad's insufficient profession of faith. Satan would change the statement by wording it as a question: *Did he take care of that a long time ago?*" I am not kidding when I say I was tortured by the devil over my dad's profession of faith. Had I done enough? Should I have shared the gospel more? Should I have probed deeper with him? Finally I had a very poignant, frank discussion with Satan. I said, "Satan, my earthly father is in the hands of my Sovereign God and Father, who is just and loving. He will judge my earthly father fairly, and this issue is completely out of my hands. I give my dad completely over to my Lord. Now leave me alone!" After that rebuke, I have never been bothered again by the eternal destiny of my dad.

CHAPTER 6

Take Time to Listen to God

God clearly speaks through our circumstances, both good and bad, whether produced by our unwise choices—even our sinful choices—or by being a victim of circumstances. Even if it comes by someone else's sinfulness or foolishness, we can still find ourselves questioning, "How in the world did I end up like this?" The word *circumstance* comes from two Latin root words meaning "around" and "to stand." So our circumstances, both good and bad, are those things that stand around us. The circumstances can be good, and sometimes crushing. Circumstances may be because of your own choices and sin, or by nothing of your own doing. I know that there are many who suffer today as a result of their circumstances and need relief and help and deliverance from their current issues. I found that my only chance to make it through the difficult seasons of life was in seeking Jesus, who never leaves us or forsakes us, as outlined in Hebrews 13:5 (NKJV). I may not ever know why my circumstances had to happen the way they did, but I do know the One who provides the way through, and that is the Holy Spirit who indwells us. The Holy Spirit is the power of God to provide the ability to live above, and eventually in victory over, our circumstances. Without the Holy Spirit you have no power over the work of the enemy of your soul, the world, the lust of the flesh, and the pride of life (1 John 2:16 NKJV). I have learned when my circumstances turn unfavorable that I must slow down and take time before the Lord. Take the time to listen to God. It is in the quiet times before Him that we can find wisdom for our lives.

You might be asking, how does this happen? It is also the Holy Spirit that allows us to walk in power from on high with our Lord. Jesus said in John 10:27 (NKJV), "My sheep hear My voice, and I know them, and they follow me." Yes, we can hear from God. We should seek God and His guidance and help in our times of need. God speaks through several different avenues, but He uses difficult things of life to get our attention. He will speak through His Word, the Bible. He will speak through your pastor or a trusted Christ follower, or even a healthcare professional. But our quiet prayer time is also a time where we can hear His yet still, small voice. In fact, God uses the difficult seasons of life, hoping we will take extra time to seek Him. The Bible says that we can know, in 1 John 5:13 (NKJV), "These things I have written to you who believe in the name of the Son of God, that you may know that you have eternal life, and that you may continue to believe in the name of the Son of God." Know that the Holy Spirit lives in you, residing in you, giving you supernaturally what you need for wisdom and life to rise above your circumstances. Just like anything else we do in life, it can take time to learn and grow to develop the attentive hearing of His yet still, small voice. When a child learns to walk, they don't just attempt the skill one time and are successful. No, they need to try and try again, and eventually learn to master the skill of balance, which leads to successfully walking, and eventually running.

Learning a new skill can require us to invest time with the scriptures and to learn from our Teacher, the Holy Spirit. We are not alone; we have a Teacher. So, don't be discouraged; keep seeking the Lord in your life and invest the time with Him. See the relationship the Lord works in you while He works out the circumstances for your good and His glory. If you are hearing this for possibly the first time about God speaking, and having a relationship with Him, and Him wanting to help you—there is a prerequisite to hearing from God in our circumstances. We all need to be in a personal relationship with Him. We need to be willing to acknowledge our need for a Savior and ask Him to come into our lives and forgive our sin, and to be filled with the Holy Spirit. It was sin that separated God from Adam and Eve in the garden. Because God is righteous and just, He cannot tolerate sin. God required that Adam and Eve depart from the garden and from His presence. God demands righteousness in order to be in a relationship with Him, and it is this same God who also provides us with the solution to our sin issue, providing the forgiveness we need to enter into a living relationship with our God through Jesus Christ. Once we say yes to Jesus, God the Father sees us through the cross and sees us as righteous. It was sin that caused my life to be filled with fear, anxiety, and eventually tragedy. It was the sin of alcoholism, drug addiction, and the pride of life. Dennis was not going to repent, no matter what. Dennis wanted to do what he wanted to do and when he wanted to do it, no matter what wise thing any other person would say. He never listed to authority. I know firsthand the pain and the tragedy that sin causes. 1 John 1:8 (NKJV) says, "If we say that we have no sin, we deceive ourselves, and the truth is not in us." Then the very next verse, 1 John 1:9, proclaims, "If we confess our sins, He (Jesus) is faithful and just to forgive us our sins and to cleanse us from all unrighteousness."

God the Father, who requires punishment for sin and eternal separation from Him, also provided the way to be forgiven by sending His Son to earth to live and eventually die, shedding His blood, which satisfied all of the sins of mankind. If you are not sure about your personal relationship with God, I have "good news" for you. We can settle this issue here and now. Do you remember when I mentioned in my story, back in chapter two, that I really had no knowledge of God and who He was? I knew that God was someone the Bible talked about, but I did not know anything about Him. It was the afternoon in my bedroom when my heart cried out, "God if you are real, you need to reveal yourself to me," because I did not want to live my life any longer. Thankfully, this prayer God honored, and I was introduced to Jesus through the youth group leader, Mrs. L. Our hope is not based on our circumstances turning around. Our hope needs to be focused on the God who loves us and has the ability to turn our circumstances around, all for His glory and ultimately our good. I had no one to tell me this so many years ago as I sat in my bedroom, feeling so hopeless, wanting to die. I was desperate for relief from my circumstances to the point of not wanting to live anymore. You may think you have the power to change things, but really, we have no power in ourselves to change. We were a slave to sin, Romans 6:17 (NKJV) tells us.

I am here to tell you that Jesus is the game-changer. John 3:16 (NJKV) says, "For God so loved the world that He (God) gave His only begotten Son (Jesus), that whoever believes in Him (Jesus) should not perish but have everlasting life." The next verse, John 3:17, goes on to say, "For God did not send His Son (Jesus) into the world to condemn the world, but that the world through Him (Jesus) might be saved." You see, Jesus' entire mission when He came to earth was not to condemn us any longer, because sin had already condemned us. Jesus came to take away the condemnation through His shed blood on the cross. I used to ask myself when I first heard the salvation story: How can the shedding of Jesus' blood pay for all of mankind's sins? The answer is found in Romans 5:19 (NKJV), "For as by one man's disobedience (sin) many were made sinners, so also by one Man's obedience many will be made righteous." It's through Jesus' blood applied to my sins that I receive the forgiveness of sins and enter into a relationship with God, which then brings the Holy Spirit to dwell inside me (Hebrews 12:1 NKJV). A life not freed from sin is a life in bondage to it (Proverbs 5:22 NKJV). That was the reason God sent His Son, Jesus Christ, to this world—to pay the penalty for our sins. Jesus' death on the cross freed mankind from the bondage of sin. "For He (God) made Him (Jesus) who knew no sin to be sin for us, that we might become the righteousness of God in Him" (2

Corinthians 5:21 NKJV). When Jesus hung on the cross, He was a willing participant. He willingly took our punishment upon Himself and died so that you and I can live in a personal relationship with God the Father. The great exchange on the cross was: Jesus took our sin, and we were given the righteousness of God. Righteousness means right standing. Jesus provided through His shed blood a right standing before God the Father.

What kind of love did it take for Jesus to do that for you and for me? How much does He love you? Romans 5:8 (NKJV), "But God demonstrates His own love toward us, in that while we were still sinners, Christ died for us." Romans 6:23 (NKJV), "For the wages of sin is death, but the gift of God is eternal life in Jesus Christ our Lord." The good news of Jesus Christ is the greatest love story ever demonstrated, and He invites you to receive His forgiveness of all sins, setting you free and providing a personal relationship with acceptance (1 Timothy 1:15 NKJV), joy, and peace, abounding in hope, by the power of the Holy Spirit (Romans 15:13 NKJV). God spoke very clearly on March 25, 1973, when Mrs. L shared that the gift of salvation belonged to me and that Jesus had put my name on it. I am here writing this book to tell you that the same gift is for you, and it has your name on it too. But when is that gift really yours? I can say it's yours. Jesus has placed your name on the gift and is holding it out to you. But when is that gift really yours? It is not yours until you reach out and take that gift. Do you believe that gift is for you? My prayer is that you do. If you believe that gift is for you, just reach out to God right now and receive that gift of salvation by faith, in Jesus' name. It's done with a simple prayer. Prayer is simply us speaking to God.

This next prayer is only an example, and you can add your personal, intimate details. I would invite you to pray this prayer and receive your gift of salvation, and change your life and circumstances for all of eternity. "God, I confess that I have sinned, and that my sin separates me from You. The Bible tells me that Jesus shed His blood on the cross and died in my place. Jesus, thank You for taking my sin upon Yourself and taking my punishment that I deserved, and in return, giving me Your righteousness. Where sin once reigned, now Your righteousness reigns, and because of what You did, I have a right standing before our heavenly Father. As an act of faith, believing that what Jesus did was for me, I am taking Your gift of salvation by faith. Come into my life, Jesus, and be my Lord and Savior. Thank You for Your amazing grace, which makes me a child of God. Thank You, Jesus. Amen."

That simple prayer of confession—that you are a sinner in need of a Savior—is prayed by faith, believing that what Jesus did so many Easters ago, He did for you. It will change you, not only while you walk this earth, but for all of eternity. It is through that simple prayer that your spirit is made alive in the Holy Spirit, and He takes up residence in you. "Now may the God of hope fill you with all joy and peace in believing, that you may abound in hope by the power of the Holy Spirit" (Romans 15:13 NKJV). If you prayed a prayer similar to this, whether a long time ago or just now, reading this book, God has heard and has sent His Holy Spirit to reside in you, which is the power that we spoke of at the beginning of this chapter. "In Him you also trusted, after you heard the word of truth, the gospel of your salvation; in whom also, having believed, you were sealed with the Holy Spirit of promise" (Ephesians 1:13 NKJV). The Holy Spirit is the right voice to lead you into truth and help you understand the scriptures. The yet still, small voice of God will never contradict the Word of God, the Bible. There have been many times when I have been discouraged by the thoughts and impressions of the enemy. If he can only get you into unbelief, he can cause chaos to reign instead of hope and peace. I will unpack that further in the next chapter; until then, I rejoice in your testimony of salvation, because now you have the foundation for power from on high to live above your circumstances. This is the first step in true triumph over the tragedies in life. The hope we all need every day, especially in the difficult seasons we are required to go through, is only found while walking with our Lord and asking Him to provide our strength for today and hope for tomorrow, and taking the time to discover and rest in Him. I am the first to say that that is not always our experience, but what I will say is that the Holy Spirit is the power for all who believe. And if you asked Jesus into your heart, you have the Holy Spirit living in you.

If you feel stuck in your same situation and God does not seem to be doing anything, pray and ask God, what is He attempting to do in you? Continue to pray; ask Him to deliver you through and from whatever your circumstances are. God has not abandoned you, but is living in you, and Hebrews 13:5 (NKJV) says, "I will never leave you nor forsake you." So, if God should happen to feel distant, it was not Him who walked away—and He gives us all the perfect opportunity to repent and change direction in our lives. The word repent in the original Greek is metanoeo, which simply means to think differently or to reconsider. I don't know about you, but I repent every day. I change my mind and reconsider and think differently. Maybe I said something or acted a certain way, and that caused someone to feel hurt because of my insensitive words or actions. Or maybe it's our attitude toward our spouse, a child, or a family relative. There are times, possibly, when we could be angry with God for not responding quickly enough to our needs. Just repent and change your mind, and if you draw close to God, He will draw close to you, as outlined in James 4:8 (NKJV). The truth is that Jesus Christ was always there, in our lives, just waiting for us to reconsider our actions and/or emotions. Once you reconsider and think differently, and repent, you may realize that Jesus and the Holy Spirit are right where they always were, and that it was your repentance that made you mindful of their rightful place and position in your life.

CHAPTER 7

The Victory in Warfare

I mentioned before that I prayed for my family for twelve years with no change, seemingly with God not showing up and answering my prayers in a way that changed my circumstances and delivered my family from a life of bondage to sin. As a result, prayer became very difficult, and I actually stopped talking to God at one point because things only seemed to get worse. I began to believe the lies of the devil that he spoke into my mind, and that was that God will answer my prayers for someone else, but He will not answer my prayers for my family because I do not deserve it—because I and my family were such bad sinners, underserving of God answering my prayers. My unbelief stemmed from my immaturity in my faith and lack of understanding of the scriptures. I did not have a strong, biblical view of God's Word and how He wants to work in us and through us through our prayers. This wrong thinking and believing did not happen right away; it took many years of praying without seeing resolution.

Because of the many years of not seeing God move in my life on behalf of my family, I allowed my circumstances to eventually take over and lead my faith instead of letting my faith lead me in my circumstances. If and when you find yourself in the deep waters of a trial, your first defense should be to seek a pastor or close friend of faith who will pray with you. Isolation is a tactic of the devil. So, your first line of defense is always to pray and ask the Holy Spirit to send you someone to walk alongside you and to come into agreement in your prayers. The next thing I will always encourage is prayer in asking for God's supernatural wisdom. Being able to discern what is actually going on in the underlying emotions and will of the individuals involved in your circumstances is an advantage only God's wisdom can provide. If you ask God for wisdom, He said in James 1:5 (NKJV), "If any of you lacks wisdom, let him ask of God, who gives to all liberally and without reproach, and it will be given to him."

Let me give you an example: if your marriage is under attack, and you're asking for God's intervention to repair your relationship and to endure under intense criticism by your spouse, godly wisdom can provide you with the understanding of what needs are required to be addressed to bring healing and lasting forgiveness and restoration. Yes, wisdom speaks to the depth of His grace and love. If you feel unloved, wisdom tells you not to look to individuals for what God intended for you to look to Him to provide in the difficult situations. Seek Him and remain in His love for you first, so you can place your own wellbeing on solid ground.

Whether God chooses to answer immediately or takes decades and even a lifetime to answer, He hears our cries and heartfelt petitions and deeply cares for us all. But to be frank, God's purpose for allowing hardship and struggles to occur in your life will always trump your desire for getting out of your current circumstance. I remember saying to myself, why doesn't God love me? Why is He not answering me? I know now that He was answering, but He was working in me for a greater purpose, and He was bringing me through the difficulty. Why did Dennis not shoot me? God said *no!* Why did Dennis not kill my mother? God said *no!* Why did God send an angel to pull me back, when I wanted to jump on Dennis and disarm him? Because God's sovereign will was that He did not want me to stop what was about to happen. These conclusions, I believe, happened the way they did by the sovereignty of God. The word *sovereignty* means supreme reign. God is the supreme, just ruler of all the heavens and earth.

When God created the earth and everything in it, He said it was good (Genesis 1:25 NKJV). It was mankind's sin that corrupted God's original plan and brought death into creation (Romans 6:23 NKJV). At the time of my trials, God's sovereignty gave little comfort in the midst of my trials, but God's involvement and supreme reign over our lives, our tragedies, and our triumphs of life do work together for good. Ultimately, it is all for His glory, and eventually our good, as Romans 8:28 tells us. There is one book of the Bible that taught me some very deep truths about God, in living in and through the difficult seasons of life. That book is the book of Job. In this book, the Holy Spirit was able to communicate a very fundamental truth to me. I went from thinking that I was at fault for my family's tragedies because I was so sinful and unworthy of the answer to my prayers, to knowing that we have an adversary who sets himself up against us and wants to destroy our faith and ultimately our lives.

In Job chapters one and two, we get a very clear picture that Satan sets out every day to accuse us before our God, and his only purpose is to kill, steal, and destroy anything that belongs to God. Revelation 12:10b (NKJV), "For the accuser of our brethren, who accused them before our God day and night, has been cast down." In Job 1:8 there is a conversation where God addresses Satan: "Then the LORD said to Satan, 'Have you considered My servant Job, that there is none like him on the earth, a blameless and upright man, one who fears God and shuns evil?'" Here, God is leading the conversation and testifying and taking delight in Job. God is really celebrating Job's faith! I feel very strongly that God does the same for you and me as well. God celebrates what faith we have and is always working for us in His sovereign will to increase our faith. Our faith is most increased in our suffering, because it is then that we need to exercise it the most. It does not take Satan long to respond in chapter one, verses 9-11 (NKJV), "So Satan answered the LORD and said, 'Does Job fear God for nothing? Have You not made a hedge around him, around his household, and around all that he has on every side? You have blessed the work of his hands, and his possessions have increased in the land. But now, stretch out Your hand and touch all that he has, and he will surely curse You to Your face!'" Here, Satan is accusing Job of not having genuine faith—that Job only honors God because everything is going well and God is blessing him. There is a very real parallel to our own lives. Do we only honor God when everything is going well, or can we also glorify our God in the tragedies or the difficult seasons of life?

God responds to Satan in chapter one, verse twelve: "Behold, all that he has is in your power; only do not lay a hand on his person." Job endured the loss of all of his children and property. He was stripped of everything but his wife. Yet after all this grief was inflicted on Job, his response was that of faith. "Then Job arose, tore his robe, and shaved his head; and he fell to the ground and worshiped. And he said: 'Naked I came from my mother's womb, and naked shall I return there. The LORD gave, and the LORD has taken away; blessed be the name of the LORD.' In all this Job did not sin nor charge God with wrong" (Job 1:20-22 NKJV). This first trial would be enough for anyone's lifetime, but Satan is relentless, and it was not enough. It's recorded in Job chapter two that Satan returns to the throne room of God, and the conversation continues about Job and starts out with God addressing Satan: "Where did you come from?" "Satan answered the LORD and said, 'From going to and fro on the earth, and from walking back and forth on it'" (Job 2:2 NKJV). Then, the Lord began to praise his servant Job for his response to his tragedy that was delivered by the hand of Satan: "Have you considered my servant Job, that there is none like him on the earth, a blameless and upright man, one who fears God and shuns evil? And still he holds fast to his integrity, although you incited Me against him, to destroy him without cause" (Job 2:3 NKJV). It did not take the accuser of the brethren long to respond to God's delight, as recorded for us in Job 2:4 (NKJV): "So Satan answered the LORD and said, 'Skin for skin! Yes, all that a man has he will give for his life. But stretch out your hand now, and touch his bone and his flesh, and he will surely curse you to your face!'" Here again, God addressed Satan's accusations about Job and allowed Satan to test Job further. "And the LORD said to Satan, 'Behold, he is in your hand, but spare his life'" (Job 2:6 NKJV).

Notice that God did and does place parameters on the test, and Satan can only function under God's supreme reign as He allows. God set boundaries for the enemy, and clearly Satan was told that he could not take Job's life. Then the Bible records in Job 2:7 (NKJV) that Satan immediately left the presence of the Lord and struck Job's body. It is my feeling that Satan could not inflict harm to Job quickly enough, because he left the presence of God immediately, and Job was given painful boils all over his body. To add insult to injury, the only family left in Job's corner was his wife, and her response in verse nine was anything but encouraging. She said, "Do you still hold on to your integrity? Curse God and die!" Job responded in verse ten and said, "'You speak as one of the foolish women... Shall we indeed accept good from God, and shall we not accept adversity?' In all this Job did not sin with his lips." I need you to notice that Job did not sin with his lips. He confessed truth in spite of the pain. I know he felt the same way his wife felt, because in Job chapter three Job was lamenting and cursing the day he was born.

These are all real emotions that go along with suffering and difficult trials. This was a very real part of my experience, and possibly yours too. No matter what the trial is, or what you have come through, we need to seek the Holy Spirit to minister truth and defeat the lies the enemy brings. Let's take a brief look back at Job chapters one and two to discover further insight. Here is real truth about the enemy and his ability, and how he works or can't work. Our God, who created everything, is omnipresent, which means He is everywhere at once, and Satan is not. That is clearly pointed out for us in Job when God askes Satan, "From where do you come?" He responds, "From going to and fro on the earth." Satan cannot be everywhere at once, so he needs his legion of fallen angels, called demons, to do his bidding. When someone asks me if I believe in ghosts, my response is yes, but you need to call them what they truly are. They are angels and demons. Angels were created by God, to serve God. Satan, along with one third of the angels, was cast out of heaven to the earth (Revelation 12:9 NKJV). Both are powerful, created beings: one for good—workers of light; and the other for evil—workers of darkness (but who can easily masquerade as an angel of light). That is why we need the Holy Spirit to guide us into all truth. Whether we realize it or not, we deal with an unseen world that we should not fear, because we have an advocate: the third part of the Trinity, the

Holy Spirit, who testifies the truth through His yet still, small voice and interprets the scriptures and testifies truth to us—and when He needs to, dispatches His angels to minister to us.

In John 14:6 (NKJV) it speaks of truth being a Person, and that Person is the Lord Jesus Christ. When you hear from God, whether in a prompting or an impression in your soul, it will never contradict the written Word of God, the Bible. The next thing we notice is that Satan does not have any issue with standing in the throne room of God. This fact really made me think. I was told that Satan could not stay where God was, because God is holy, and Satan cannot be in God's presence and has to flee. While that may be true in some cases where he is cast out, here in Job chapters one and two, Satan not only stands in the throne room of God but holds a conversation with the God of all creation. The reason Satan seeks to converse with God is to accuse us. One of Satan's names recorded in scriptures is "the accuser of the brethren," found in Revelation 12:10 (NKJV). Once Satan accuses Job, he seeks permission to test Job. Notice that Satan cannot do anything without permission. Satan has no power over God. How can creation ever stand above or demand from its Creator? The answer is, it cannot! Our God is the Creator of everything, and He said it was good. I hope this disarms his accusing voice in your mind. Reject his lies and hold on to the truth. Sin will take you farther and deeper than you ever thought and cost you more than you can ever pay.

This is true for everyone, especially if you are a Christ follower. Satan and his legions of demons will do whatever they can to render your faith useless and hopeless, and get you off of your identity in Jesus Christ and onto your circumstances, onto relationships, onto material things. He will challenge your understanding of the scriptures and attack your very identity as a believer in Jesus Christ and His forgiveness and love for you. He will do whatever it takes to keep you from walking by faith, and to get you back on your circumstances. Satan will even use scripture, and change it just a little bit, to feed your flesh. He may not be able to take away your salvation, but he wants to take you out of God's perfect will and drop you into the gutter of despair and hopelessness. However, walking and abiding in the power of the Holy Spirit, we have all we need for the victory. Ephesians 6:10-13 (NKJV) tells us, "Finally, my brethren, be strong in the Lord and in the power of His might. Put on the whole armor of God, that you may be able to stand against the wiles of the devil. For we do not wrestle against flesh and blood, but against principalities, against powers, against the rulers of the darkness of this age, against spiritual hosts of wickedness in the heavenly places. Therefore take up the whole armor of God, that you may be able to withstand in the evil day, and having done all, to stand." This is a real spiritual battle for the hearts and souls of mankind. If nothing else at the end of the battle, "having done all, to stand." Let me ask the question: If you fight a battle, and you're still standing at the end of that battle, is that not a good thing? Praise the Lord that after all I have been asked to go through, I am still standing, and my faith is steadfast and sure in my God and Savior Jesus Christ.

God certainly does know when trials are coming our way. God does not tempt us, but will allow temptation and trials; but He does not abandon us is our time of need. Jesus tells Peter, in Luke 22, that he is headed for a trial at the hands of Satan. "And the Lord said, 'Simon, Simon! Indeed, Satan has asked for you, that he may sift you as wheat. But I have prayed for you, that your faith should not fail; and when you have returned to Me, strengthen your brethren'" (Luke 22:31-32 NKJV). Have you thought about why the word *sift* is used here? I would watch my grandmother sift flour, and it was a process where you refined the flour to a smoother consistency to make it better for whatever you wanted to use it for. I believe God used a generic word for Peter's testing so that we can apply this verse to our own experience. Think about this question. Has Satan gone to God and asked to sift you as wheat? Let's look at Jesus' response in verse 32, which is not a generic response. Jesus was not going to stop what was about to happen, but was allowing Satan to sift Peter. But Jesus does not abandon Peter and prays that his faith may remain, and then tells him after coming through, to go and strengthen his fellow believers. In other words, encourage others with the encouragement you have been given. It is in the difficult times and seasons of life that we get to see the faithfulness of our God.

At the end of Job's trial, he says in chapter 42:5 (NKJV), "I have heard of You by the hearing of the ear, but now my eye sees You." Job's intense suffering took Job to a deeper relationship and knowledge of who his God is. Job now doesn't just hear his God; as a result of what has happened, he now sees his God. God has a reason in the difficulties. He wants us to demonstrate faith, and through faith give opportunity for real intimacy to grow in our relationship with Him. What I mean by intimacy is closeness, familiarity, affinity with your Savior. Jesus wants you to not only hear Him, but He wants all of us to also see Him. He longs to be in an intimate relationship with us. The flip side is that the enemy wants us to think just the opposite. To think of our suffering as punishment, or to question God's ability to help us, or to doubt His love and affection toward us. It took some time of continuing in God's Word and seeking wise council, and time walking with the Lord, to bring the growth and understanding that the testing of my faith through my trials served a greater purpose, and the writing of this book is just one of the greater purposes. This book is more than I could have ever imagined. Another was the years I have had encouraging others with the encouragement I was shown as a result of my relationship with Jesus Christ, and the truth and power imparted to me by the Holy Spirit. That is the true triumph over the tragedy, and I have found Him faithful.

CHAPTER 8

Persistence in Prayer

I always thought that prayer was pretty straightforward. It's me talking to God in a reverent, formal setting, informing Him about everything I need in my life. You ask God for something, and eventually, whatever you ask for is provided. It's almost like we think of God as a genie, where we get all the wishes we want. In reality, we can be disheartened pretty quickly when our requests go seemingly unanswered. Have you have ever prayed for God to respond to a desperate need in your life, and He is just not showing up or bringing the relief or answers you need? Praying over and over for the same things can seem useless or even hopeless. Persistence easily wanes in prolonged seasons of unanswered prayers. The struggle is very real to stay engaged in consistent and powerful prayer. I have found that what is needed to be persistent in our prayer time requires a few prerequisites. It requires us to stay immersed in the scriptures, which lead us in our walk and fellowship with the Holy Spirit, along with attending a local, Bible-teaching gathering of believers in Jesus, "the church." The Bible instructs us in Hebrews 10:24-25 (NKJV), "And let us consider one another in order to stir up love and good works, not forsaking the assembling of ourselves together, as is the manner of some, but exhorting one another, and so much the more as you see the Day approaching."

This is important because when we are connected, we are encouraged in the process of the renewing of our minds, as is told in 2 Corinthians 4:16 (NKJV): "Therefore we do not lose heart. Even though our outward man is perishing, yet the inward man is being renewed day by day." 1 Thessalonians 5:16-18 (NKJV) call us to pray without ceasing: "Rejoice always, pray without ceasing, in everything give thanks; for this is the will of God in Christ Jesus for you." We need the scriptures and each other the most when our circumstances become increasingly more difficult and go beyond what we think we can handle or should have to endure. God did not instruct us to gather together because He needed it. In fact, He knew in His perfect will that we would need each other much more as we progress in our relationship with Christ. When the church gathers together, it's for us the worshiper as much as it is for us to worship. It's where we realign our thinking and identity with the Lord in a safe place, to love and be loved, and to encourage and be encouraged, so we can press forward by faith unto good works for the glory of God. Unfortunately, the first attack from Satan is to cause us to isolate ourselves. When we isolate ourselves and remove ourselves from the fellowship of the church, we play right into the enemy's game plan. Separating ourselves only takes us further down the road of unbelief, which enhances our fears and brings on hopelessness and despair, and weakens us further in our struggle. We need each other by God's design.

In my case, as I mentioned in the last chapter, because my prayers had gone unanswered for so long, I thought I was being punished. The lie of punishment was the first step in Satan's deception, bringing me to my hopelessness, which caused me to pull back and not engage any further. How did that unbelief take place? It is simple. It was in my thinking, which was grounded on emotion and half-truths rather than "the truth." In my thinking, I thought: God is love, He is all powerful, He can do all things, and I have prayed and asked Him to change my circumstances by changing the hearts of my family through salvation. Yet nothing has changed, and it has only gotten worse. So why am I praying? This must be happening because I am a bad person, and God is not answering or even hearing my prayers because of my sin and the sins of my family. I must be receiving His just response because of my sin. The conclusion in my mind was: God is never at fault and certainly is not broken, so therefore it must be me who is at fault and me who is broken. Therefore, I am reaping what I deserve. My wrong thinking led me to think that somehow, I needed to pay for the sins of my family. Because my thinking was wrong, it led me to wrong belief and unbelief. The hopelessness that flowed from the lies kept me from seeking the truth and kept me from fellowship, which was the remedy for my situation. Captive, I weaved in and out of my experience until I overcame my pride and shame and reached out for help from a pastor. I encourage anyone who is in a downward spiral to do the same. I am sure that my deception is not an isolated case, and if the devil convinced me, he certainly will be attempting to convince many others of the same unbelief in our true identity in Jesus Christ, in the hopes of rendering them ineffective and causing hopelessness to reign in their lives.

We can never measure faith by our experience. Instead, we need our experience to be continually measured by our faith. The harder our experience, the more faith we need to overcome. How do we get more faith? Paul again writes in Romans 10:17 (NKJV), "So then faith comes by hearing, and hearing by the word of God." Hebrews 12:2a (NKJV) says, "Looking unto Jesus, the author and finisher of our faith." Unbelief and wrong believing will never produce anything but wrong living. It was this wrong believing that shipwrecked my desire to continue to pray. The only way to turn this thinking around was by renewing my mind with truth from the scriptures that supply us with our new identity, and our adoption into the family of God, through faith. When we enter a relationship with Christ Jesus, we also become an heir and co-heir with Christ. We are told in Romans 8:17 (NKJV), "And if children, then heirs—heirs of God and joint heirs with Christ, if indeed we suffer with Him, that we may also be glorified together." We now get to call our heavenly Father "Abba," which when translated means "Daddy." God is not a staunch deity sitting in His throne room, just waiting for us to make a mistake so He can punish us. We read in Galatians 4:5-7 (NKJV), "To redeem those who were under the law, that we might receive the adoption as sons. And because you are sons, God has sent forth the Spirit of His Son into your hearts, crying out, 'Abba, Father!' Therefore you are no longer a slave but a son, and if a son, then an heir of God through Christ." The intimacy we now have in our relationship with our Daddy, God, was only possible because of the obedience of the one, Jesus, who died so that we can be in relationship with our Daddy. What earthly daddy doesn't want to give good things to his children? All the more so for our heavenly Daddy; wouldn't He want to give us good things? In Matthew

7:11 (NKJV) it says, "If you then, being evil, know how to give good gifts to your children, how much more will your Father who is in heaven give good things to those who ask Him!"

It was necessary for me to sit and take time to read and understand Jesus, and His message of love and grace that He extended toward me personally. I want to encourage you to pursue His love for you—the same love He demonstrated by His willingness to die on the cross for you and me. It is that same love, when fully understood, that conquers the fear that so easily paralyzes us in life, thwarting the work of God in our hearts. God's Word in 1 John 4:18 (NKJV) says, "There is no fear in love; but perfect love casts out fear, because fear involves torment. But he who fears has not been made perfect in love." There is no shortcut to the reality of the depth of His love, except praying and asking the Holy Spirit to reveal the deeper mysteries of Jesus' love toward us. That alone, if revealed, will keep you and me in pursuit of the fullness of God in our lives and keep us from the paralyzing effects of fear. I am so thankful for everything God has revealed and done through it all, but I have come to the conclusion that it has more to do with the revelation of how much He loves me, and less to do with how much I love Him. His love is what transforms the heart, because it is the goodness of God that leads us to repentance, according to Romans 2:4 (NKJV).

These next verses in Ephesians are my heart's prayer for everyone who desires to go deeper with the Lord. Ephesians 3:17-20 (NKJV): "That Christ may dwell in your hearts through faith; that you, being rooted and grounded in love, may be able to comprehend with all the saints what is the width and length and depth and height—to know the love of Christ which passes knowledge; that you may be filled with all the fullness of God. Now to Him who is able to do exceedingly abundantly above all that we ask or think, according to the power that works in us, to Him be glory in the church by Christ Jesus to all generations, forever and ever. Amen." Let's claim the promises for that truth and renew our minds continually with the truth of His love for us. It's then that we can continue to pursue God and be faithful and persistent in our prayers, and all for His glory in our lives, and eventually our good. Amen and amen.

CHAPTER 9

Triumph

I surmise that it's been the better part of two decades since I sensed the prompting of the Lord to write this book, telling my story. In the delay of writing the book, I wrestled with the idea; did I really hear or sense God calling me to write my story? I wasn't looking forward to hashing through all the bad memories and reliving the tragedy that I have tried so hard to forget. Brenda would remind me at various times that I needed to do as I was told and write the book. As I look back, I think the delay was by design, and is just what God wanted—and that the timing of this writing is right on time and will accomplish the purpose for which He wants it. I am not a noted author, but just a man who wants you to hear my story and say that if God brought Dale through so much, He will do it for you too.

My aspiration is that through my story you will receive encouragement and hope, dispel the lies of the enemy, and encourage a desire to dive deeper in discovering the mysteries of the Savior's love for you and your family. He wants to provide everything you need to be victorious in this life, as well as to overcome death and the grave to everlasting life (Hosea 13:14, and Romans 5:21, and John 3:16 NKJV). You don't have to be in tragedy to come to Him. Just come as you are and tell Him the desires of your heart, knowing that He is God, the Supreme Ruler over all creation, and that He hears us. Why does He hear us? Because of His love for us. Don't let the enemy ever convince you of any other truth.

Throughout my life I can testify that God has never abandoned me. In the seasons of life where it became difficult, and I struggled with depression and anxiety, it may have felt that way; but we can't rely on our feelings—we must rely on truth. Feelings are unstable and are all over the place and subject to change at a moment's notice. The truth for life comes from the Bible, and the Bible records for us in John 8:32 (NKJV), "And you shall know the truth, and the truth shall make you free." Further on in the scriptures, it's written in John 14:6 (NKJV), "Jesus said to him, 'I am the way, the truth, and the life. No one comes to the Father except through Me.'" The ability to live victoriously in every season of life comes by living in a personal relationship with Jesus Christ and walking in the power of the Holy Spirit. The victory is in establishing in your heart the truth, as stated in Romans 8:31 (NIV), "What, then, shall we say in response to these things? If God is for us, who can be against us?" Who in all of creation can overcome our Creator and the Supreme Ruler of this world? No one, and our God is on our side.

The Bible also proclaims, "I can do all things through Christ who strengthens me" (Philippians 4:13 NKJV). That verse just said we can do "all things." If I had a dollar for every time I told the Lord, "I can't do it," I would be financially better off for sure. The truth is that I am not defined by my successes or my failures in life. I am defined by the One who provided a way into my successes and delivered through my failures.

Summing up everything that I've learned from my life and relationship with Jesus: our victory is more of a state of resting in Him than a state of doing. What I mean by this is, it's not who I am in my circumstances and what I can do, but whose I am, whom I belong to, and what He can do in me and through me, using my circumstances for His glory, and working it ultimately for my good. To be triumphant in life, I need to continually renew the thought in my mind that I belong to the Lord, and He will not leave me or forsake me. So that I can boldly say: "The Lord is my helper; I will not fear. What can man do to me?" (Hebrews 13:6 NKJV). Did I do it perfectly? No, but doing it perfectly is not a prerequisite for God to do His part perfectly. The Bible also says, and I am paraphrasing, that God is faithful, who will not allow you to be tempted beyond what you are able to bear, and will with any temptation provide a way of escape (1 Corinthians 10:13 NKJV).

How did I come through the trauma of having an alcoholic father, who was the sweetest person until the alcohol started to take over, and then the attempted murder of my mother before my very eyes, and then the suicides of Dennis and Doug? I am not so sure that I am not still healing as a result of writing this book. However, God has been so faithful in bringing me through the tragedies and has allowed me to triumph because He is faithful.

As I type this last chapter, in just a few days Brenda and I will be celebrating forty years of marriage. She has been such a gift to me as we have navigated life together along with the Lord. Out of all the dysfunction that I lived in and through, Brenda was and continues to be a gift from God.

It was just a short five years into our marriage when we were blessed with our oldest little bundle of joy, Christie, followed by Ashley, and then Aaron. They have grown into the most amazing young adults, and my life is so blessed because of them being in it. An additional blessing has been the young men who married my daughters, Kyle and Ray. I can't express enough the comfort it brings me, knowing that my daughters are loved and cared for by someone who loves them as I love Brenda. The most recent joy in our family was Aaron realizing the truth of Proverbs 18:22 and being united in marriage to his beautiful bride Mary, whom we adore. I cannot write about triumphs in my life without mentioning my beautiful grandchildren, Lucy, Rosalie, and Luke. They bring so much joy and love into our lives, not to mention the blessing they are to Brenda and me.

When you have a child, it really places love in perspective. When I look at my children, I just can't imagine loving anything more on this earth, and I would be willing to lay my life down so they could live. As they grew, I would tell them that I loved them. They would respond, "I love you, Dad," and my response to that was, "I love you more." I told them that there is no way they could love me as much as I love them. That last sentence is a metaphor for our relationship with God. We cannot love God as much as He loves us. Jesus laid His life down so we could live. How much love must someone have to be willing to die for someone, to provide forgiveness of sins so we can enjoy a relationship with our heavenly Father for all of eternity? How can we question God's love toward us, when He provided for us what we couldn't provide for ourselves? That's a parent's powerful love for His child, and I am here to tell you, that is the truth that always leads to triumph over tragedy. If He provided that for us, will He not continue to be faithful? I have found Him faithful.

Contact

If you would like to reach out to the author with your questions, to share a prayer request, or to share how this book might have encouraged you, you can reach me, J. Dale Alderfer, at *Alderfertragedyandtriumph@gmail.com*. I would love to hear from you and would count it a privilege to pray for you. God bless.

CPSIA information can be obtained
at www.ICGtesting.com
Printed in the USA
LVHW050209030221
678222LV00003B/503